MATH Expressions
Common Core

Dr. Karen C. Fuson

GRADE

1

Volume 1

This material is based upon work supported by the
National Science Foundation
under Grant Numbers
ESI-9816320, REC-9806020, and RED-935373.

Any opinions, findings, and conclusions, or recommendations expressed in this material
are those of the author and do not necessarily reflect the views of the National Science Foundation.

HOUGHTON MIFFLIN HARCOURT

Name _____

1. Write how many dots. See the 5 in each group.

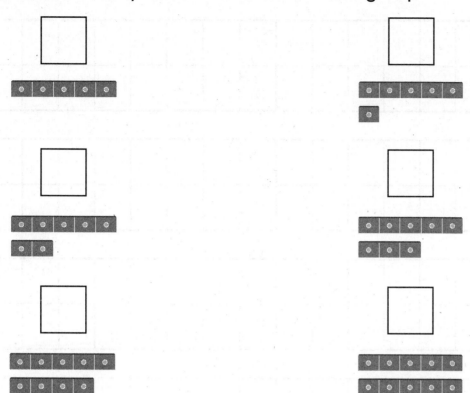

2. See the 5-group. Draw extra dots to show the number.

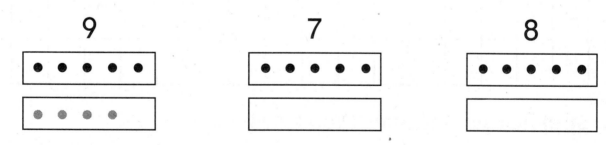

3. Write the numbers from 0–10.

0 1 2 3 4 5 6 7 8 9 10

© Houghton Mifflin Harcourt Publishing Company

Remembering

Write the numbers.

1. | 0 | 0 | 0 | | | | | | | | | | | | |
   |---|---|---|---|---|---|---|---|---|---|---|---|---|---|---|
   | 0 | | | | | | | | | | | | | | |

2. | 1 | 1 | 1 | | | | | | | | | | | | |
   |---|---|---|---|---|---|---|---|---|---|---|---|---|---|---|
   | 1 | | | | | | | | | | | | | | |

3. | 2 | 2 | 2 | | | | | | | | | | | | |
   |---|---|---|---|---|---|---|---|---|---|---|---|---|---|---|
   | 2 | | | | | | | | | | | | | | |

4. | 3 | 3 | 3 | | | | | | | | | | | | |
   |---|---|---|---|---|---|---|---|---|---|---|---|---|---|---|
   | 3 | | | | | | | | | | | | | | |

5. | 4 | 4 | 4 | | | | | | | | | | | | |
   |---|---|---|---|---|---|---|---|---|---|---|---|---|---|---|
   | 4 | | | | | | | | | | | | | | |

6. **Stretch Your Thinking** Draw 2 flowers.

Homework

Write how many dots. See the 5 in each group.

1.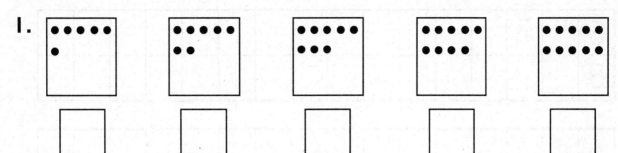

___

Write how many leaves. See the 5 in each row.

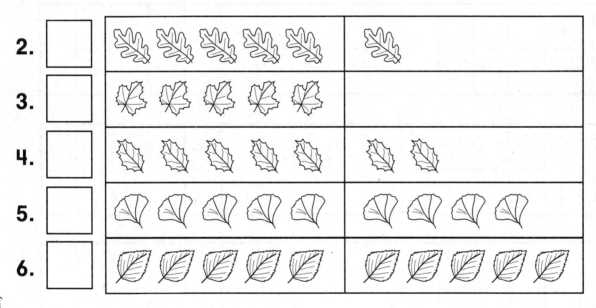

2.

3.

4.

5.

6.

___

7. Write the numbers from 0–10.

0 1 2 3 4 5 6 7 8 9 10

8. Explain to your Homework Helper how 5-groups help you see 6, 7, 8, 9, 10.

Remembering

Write the numbers.

1. | 5 | 5 | 5 | | | | | | | | | | | |
|---|---|---|---|---|---|---|---|---|---|---|---|---|---|
| 5 | | | | | | | | | | | | | |

2. | 6 | 6 | 6 | | | | | | | | | | | |
|---|---|---|---|---|---|---|---|---|---|---|---|---|---|
| 6 | | | | | | | | | | | | | |

3. | 7 | 7 | 7 | | | | | | | | | | | |
|---|---|---|---|---|---|---|---|---|---|---|---|---|---|
| 7 | | | | | | | | | | | | | |

4. | 8 | 8 | 8 | | | | | | | | | | | |
|---|---|---|---|---|---|---|---|---|---|---|---|---|---|
| 8 | | | | | | | | | | | | | |

5. | 9 | 9 | 9 | | | | | | | | | | | |
|---|---|---|---|---|---|---|---|---|---|---|---|---|---|
| 9 | | | | | | | | | | | | | |

6. **Stretch Your Thinking** Draw 3 cats.

Visualize a Number as a 5-Group and Ones

Homework

Write the partners.

1.  ● ● ● ● ○ $5 = 4 + 1$ _____

   ● ● ● ○ ○ $5 =$ _____

   ● ● ○ ○ ○ $5 =$ _____

   ● ○ ○ ○ ○ $5 =$ _____

2.

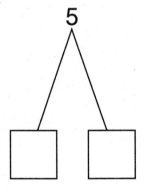
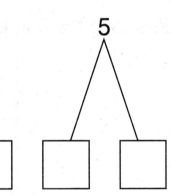

3. Write the numbers.

0	0	0												
0														

1	1	1												
1														

Remembering

Write how many airplanes. See the 5 in each row.

1. [ ] 🛩🛩🛩🛩🛩 | 🛩

2. [ ] ✈✈✈✈✈ | ✈✈✈

3. [ ] ✈✈✈✈✈

4. [ ] ✈✈✈✈✈ | ✈✈

Write how many dots. See the 5 in each group.

5. [ ]

6. [ ]

7. [ ]

8. [ ]

9. Stretch Your Thinking Draw 4 trees.

Name _____

1. Show and write the 6-partners.

○○○○○○	+	$6 =$ _____
○○○○○○	+	$6 =$ _____
○○○○○○	+	$6 =$ _____
○○○○○○	+	$6 =$ _____
○○○○○○	+	$6 =$ _____

2. Write the 6-partners.

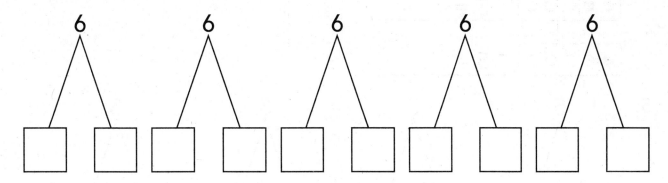

3. Write the numbers.

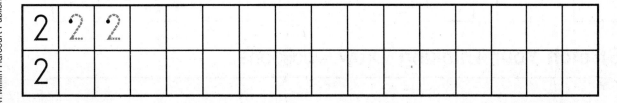

Name _____

Remembering

Write how many chickens. See the 5 in each row.

1. ☐

2. ☐

3. ☐

Write the partners.

4. ●●●●○ $5 = 4 + 1$

   ●●●○○ $5 =$ _____

   ●●○○○ $5 =$ _____

   ●○○○○ $5 =$ _____

5.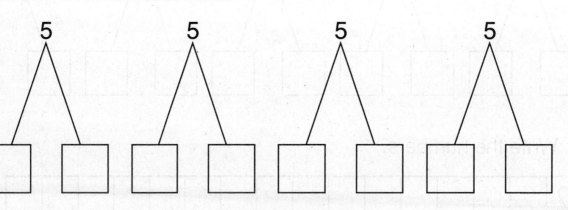

6. **Stretch Your Thinking** Draw 5 balloons.

Name _____

Homework

Show the 7-partners and switch the partners.

1. | ○○○○○○○ | | + | and | + |

2. | ○○○○○○○ | | + | and | + |

3. | ○○○○○○○ | | + | and | + |

Write the partners and the switched partners.

4.

7-train

| + | + | + |
| + | + | + |

Use patterns to solve.

5. 2 + 1 = ☐   4 + 1 = ☐   5 + 1 = ☐

6 + 1 = ☐   1 + 1 = ☐   3 + 1 = ☐

6. 1 + 6 = ☐   1 + 1 = ☐   1 + 2 = ☐

1 + 5 = ☐   1 + 4 = ☐   1 + 3 = ☐

Write the numbers.

7.

| 4 | 4 | 4 | | | | | | | | | | |
| 4 | | | | | | | | | | | | |

8.

| 5 | 5 | 5 | | | | | | | | | | |
| 5 | | | | | | | | | | | | |

Remembering

Write how many dots. See the 5 in each group.

I.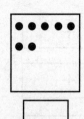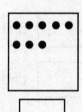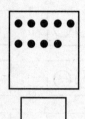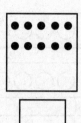

Show and write the 6-partners.

2.
⊂○○○○○○⊃ | + | 6 = _____

⊂○○○○○○⊃ | + | 6 = _____

⊂○○○○○○⊃ | + | 6 = _____

⊂○○○○○○⊃ | + | 6 = _____

⊂○○○○○○⊃ | + | 6 = _____

Add.

3. I + 0 = ☐   5 + 0 = ☐   3 + 0 = ☐

4. I + I = ☐   2 + I = ☐   4 + I = ☐

5. Stretch Your Thinking Draw 6 apples. Use a 5-group.

Name _____

Show the 8-partners and switch the partners.

1. ⬜ O O O O O O O O | [+] and [+]

2. ⬜ O O O O O O O O | [+] and [+]

3. ⬜ O O O O O O O O | [+] and [+]

4. ⬜ O O O O O O O O | [+] and [+]

Write the partners and the switched partners.

5.

8-train

[+] [+] [+] [+]
[+] [+] [+] [+]

Use patterns to solve.

6. $8 + 0 =$ ☐ $5 + 0 =$ ☐ $0 + 4 =$ ☐

$0 + 6 =$ ☐ $0 + 2 =$ ☐ $0 + 7 =$ ☐

Write the numbers.

7.

6	6	6												
6														

8.

7	7	7	7	7										
7														

Remembering

Write how many of each food. See the 5 in each row.

1. ☐

2. ☐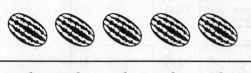

3. ☐

Show the 7-partners and switch the partners.

4. ⃝⃝⃝⃝⃝⃝⃝　☐ + ☐　and　☐ + ☐

5. ⃝⃝⃝⃝⃝⃝⃝　☐ + ☐　and　☐ + ☐

6. ⃝⃝⃝⃝⃝⃝⃝　☐ + ☐　and　☐ + ☐

7. Write the partners and the switched partners.

7-train

☐ + ☐　☐ + ☐　☐ + ☐
☐ + ☐　☐ + ☐　☐ + ☐

8. **Stretch Your Thinking** Draw 7 fish. Use a 5-group.

© Houghton Mifflin Harcourt Publishing Company

Homework

Show the 9-partners and switch the partners.

1. ⃝⃝⃝⃝⃝⃝⃝⃝⃝   [+]   and   [+]

2. ⃝⃝⃝⃝⃝⃝⃝⃝⃝   [+]   and   [+]

3. ⃝⃝⃝⃝⃝⃝⃝⃝⃝   [+]   and   [+]

4. ⃝⃝⃝⃝⃝⃝⃝⃝⃝   [+]   and   [+]

Write the partners and the switched partners.

5.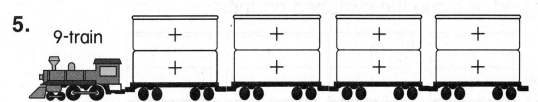

9-train   [+ / +]   [+ / +]   [+ / +]   [+ / +]

Use patterns to solve.

6. $6 - 1 = \boxed{}$ $7 - 1 = \boxed{}$ $4 - 1 = \boxed{}$

   $9 - 1 = \boxed{}$ $5 - 1 = \boxed{}$ $8 - 1 = \boxed{}$

Write the numbers.

7. | 8 | 8 | 8 | | | | | | | | | | | | |
   |---|---|---|---|---|---|---|---|---|---|---|---|---|---|---|
   | 8 | | | | | | | | | | | | | | |

8. | 9 | 9 | 9 | | | | | | | | | | | | |
   |---|---|---|---|---|---|---|---|---|---|---|---|---|---|---|
   | 9 | | | | | | | | | | | | | | |

Remembering

Show the 8-partners and switch the partners.

1. $\bigcirc\bigcirc\bigcirc\bigcirc\bigcirc\bigcirc\bigcirc\bigcirc$ ___ + ___   and   ___ + ___

2. $\bigcirc\bigcirc\bigcirc\bigcirc\bigcirc\bigcirc\bigcirc\bigcirc$ ___ + ___   and   ___ + ___

3. $\bigcirc\bigcirc\bigcirc\bigcirc\bigcirc\bigcirc\bigcirc\bigcirc$ ___ + ___   and   ___ + ___

4. $\bigcirc\bigcirc\bigcirc\bigcirc\bigcirc\bigcirc\bigcirc\bigcirc$ ___ + ___   and   ___ + ___

---

5. Write the partners and the switched partners.

8-train   ___ + ___   ___ + ___   ___ + ___   ___ + ___
          ___ + ___   ___ + ___   ___ + ___   ___ + ___

Subtract.

6. $4 - 1 = \boxed{}$ $2 - 1 = \boxed{}$ $3 - 1 = \boxed{}$

7. $2 - 2 = \boxed{}$ $5 - 2 = \boxed{}$ $3 - 2 = \boxed{}$

8. **Stretch Your Thinking** Draw 8 bugs. Use a 5-group.

Name _____

Homework

1. Write the 10-partners and the switched partners.

$\dfrac{9 + 1}{}$	$\dfrac{\quad + \quad}{}$	$\dfrac{\quad + \quad}{}$	$\dfrac{\quad + \quad}{}$	$\dfrac{\quad + \quad}{}$
$\dfrac{1 + 9}{}$	$\dfrac{\quad + \quad}{}$	$\dfrac{\quad + \quad}{}$	$\dfrac{\quad + \quad}{}$	$\dfrac{\quad + \quad}{}$

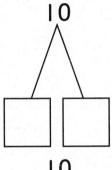
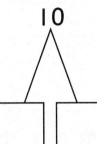
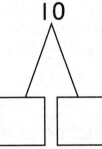
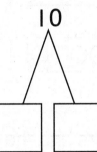
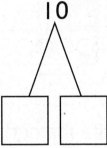

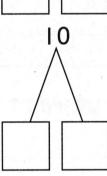
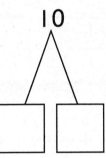
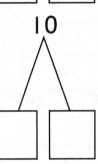
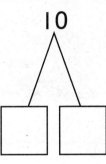

2. Use patterns to solve.

$7 + 1 = \boxed{}$	$9 + 1 = \boxed{}$	$1 + 8 = \boxed{}$
$10 - 1 = \boxed{}$	$7 - 1 = \boxed{}$	$9 - 1 = \boxed{}$
$9 + 0 = \boxed{}$	$0 + 10 = \boxed{}$	$7 + 0 = \boxed{}$
$8 - 0 = \boxed{}$	$7 - 0 = \boxed{}$	$10 - 0 = \boxed{}$

Partners of 10 **15**

Name _____

Remembering

Show the 9-partners and switch the partners.

1. ⬜ O O O O O O O O O ⬜ | ⬜ + ⬜ and ⬜ + ⬜

2. ⬜ O O O O O O O O O ⬜ | ⬜ + ⬜ and ⬜ + ⬜

3. ⬜ O O O O O O O O O ⬜ | ⬜ + ⬜ and ⬜ + ⬜

4. ⬜ O O O O O O O O O ⬜ | ⬜ + ⬜ and ⬜ + ⬜

Write the partners and the switched partners.

5.

9-train

| + | + | + | + |
| + | + | + | + |

---

6. Write the numbers from 0 – 10.

| 0 | | | 4 | | | 7 | | | |

7. **Stretch Your Thinking** Draw 9 stars. Use a 5-group.

Homework

Show and write the partners of 10.

1. ◎◎◎◎◎◎◎◎◎○ 10 = ____ + ____

2. ○○○○○○○○○○ 10 = ____ + ____

3. ○○○○○○○○○○ 10 = ____ + ____

4. ○○○○○○○○○○ 10 = ____ + ____

5. ○○○○○○○○○○ 10 = ____ + ____

6. ○○○○○○○○○○ 10 = ____ + ____

7. ○○○○○○○○○○ 10 = ____ + ____

8. ○○○○○○○○○○ 10 = ____ + ____

9. ○○○○○○○○○○ 10 = ____ + ____

Remembering

Write the 10-partners and the switched partners.

1. 　　　　　　

$$\underline{9 + 1}$$　　$$\underline{+}$$　　$$\underline{+}$$　　$$\underline{+}$$　　$$\underline{+}$$

$$1 + 9$$　　$$+$$　　$$+$$　　$$+$$　　$$+$$

2. 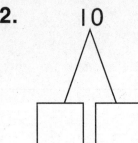　　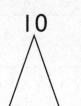　　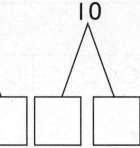

　　　　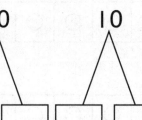

3.

4. Stretch Your Thinking Draw 10 marbles.

Use 5-groups.

Homework

Write the partners and the total.

1. 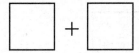 +

Total ☐

2. 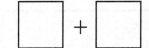 +

Total ☐

3.  + ☐

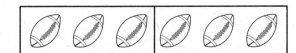

Total ☐

4.  +

Total ☐

5. ☐ + ☐

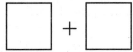

Total ☐

6. ☐ + ☐

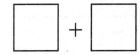

Total ☐

7. ☐ + ☐

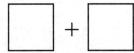

Total ☐

8. ☐ + ☐

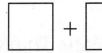

Total ☐

Represent Addition **19**

Name _____

Remembering

1. Write the numbers from 0–10.

2. Write how many dots. See the 5 in each group.

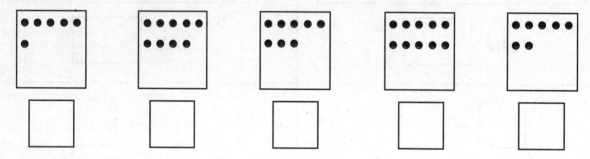

Write how many leaves. See the 5 in each row.

3.

4.

5.

6. Write the 5-partners as a train.

5-train

| + | + | + | + |

7. Stretch Your Thinking Write partners of 7. Draw a Break-Apart Stick to show the partners. Write the total.

☐ + ☐

Total ☐

Represent Addition

Homework

Name _____

Write the partners and total for each circle drawing.

1. ☐ + ☐

● ● ● ● ● ● ● | ○ ○

Total ☐

2. ☐ + ☐

● ● ● ● | ○ ○ ○

Total ☐

3. ☐ + ☐

● ● ● ● ● | ○

Total ☐

4. ☐ + ☐

● ● ● ● ● ● ● ● ● | ○ ○

Total ☐

5. ☐ + ☐

● ● ● ● | ○ ○

Total ☐

6. ☐ + ☐

● ● ● ● ● | ○ ○ ○ ○

Total ☐

7. ☐ + ☐

● ● ● ● ● ● | ○ ○ ○

Total ☐

8. ☐ + ☐

● ● ● ● ● | ○ ○ ○ ○ ○

Total ☐

Addition with Circle Drawings **21**

Remembering

1. Write how many dots. See the 5 in each group.

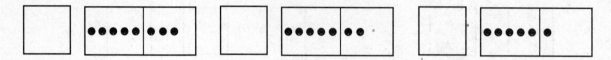

Write how many of each food. See the 5 in each row.

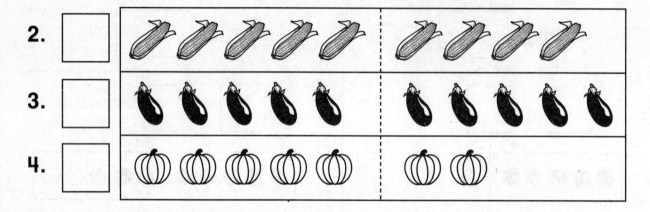

2.

3.

4.

5. Write the 6-partners as a train.

6-train

6. Stretch Your Thinking Make a circle drawing
to show a set of partners of 10.

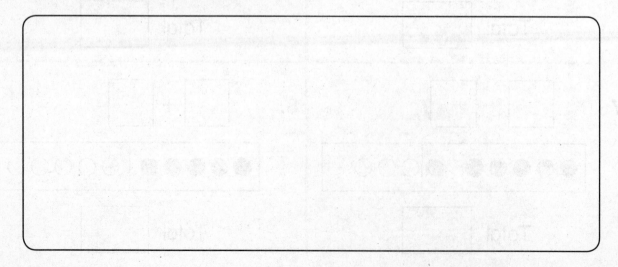

Name _____

Homework

Write the partners and the total. Then write the equation.

1. 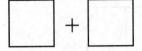 ☐ + ☐

 ●●●●● ●● ○○

_____
Equation

Total ☐

2. ☐ + ☐

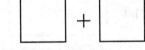 ●●●●● ○○○

_____
Equation

Total ☐

3. ☐ + ☐

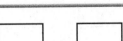 ●●●●● ● ○○○○

_____
Equation

Total ☐

4. ☐ + ☐

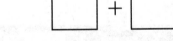 ●●●●● ○○

_____
Equation

Total ☐

Addition Equations **23**

Remembering

1. Fill in the numbers from 0–10.

0			4		7			

Show the 7-partners and switch the partners.

2. ◯◯◯◯◯◯◯   [+] and [+]

3. ◯◯◯◯◯◯◯   [+] and [+]

4. ◯◯◯◯◯◯◯   [+] and [+]

5. Write the partners and the switched partners.

7-train   [+ / +] [+ / +] [+ / +]

6. **Stretch Your Thinking** Make a circle drawing to match the picture. Then write the equation.

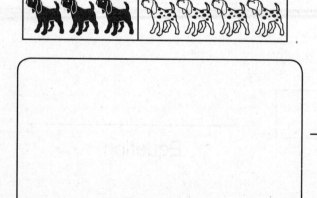

_____
Equation

Homework

Name _____

Write the partners and the total. Then write the equation.

1.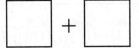

Total [ ] _____
Equation

2. [ ] + [ ]

Total [ ] _____
Equation

3. [ ] + [ ]

Total [ ] _____
Equation

4. [ ] + [ ]

Total [ ] _____
Equation

Remembering

Write how many of each food. See the 5 in each row.

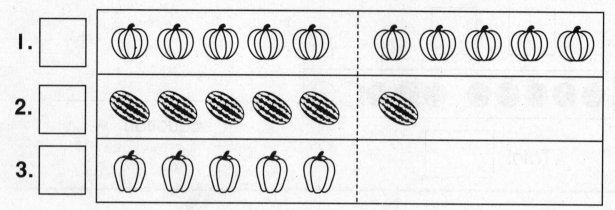

1. ☐

2. ☐

3. ☐

Show the 8-partners and switch the partners.

4. ◯◯◯◯◯◯◯◯   [+]   and   [+]

5. ◯◯◯◯◯◯◯◯   [+]   and   [+]

6. ◯◯◯◯◯◯◯◯   [+]   and   [+]

7. ◯◯◯◯◯◯◯◯   [+]   and   [+]

8. Write the partners and the switched partners.

8-train

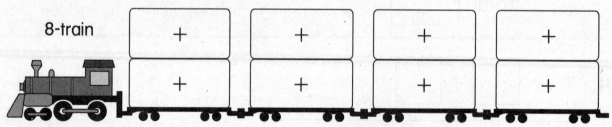

9. **Stretch Your Thinking** Write an equation to match the circle drawing.

_____
Equation

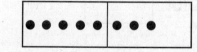

Addition Equations and Stories

Homework

Count on to find the total.

1. $6 + 3 =$ ☐   **2.** $3 + 5 =$ ☐   **3.** $4 + 5 =$ ☐

4. $5 + 5 =$ ☐   **5.** $4 + 6 =$ ☐   **6.** $2 + 4 =$ ☐

7. $4 + 3 =$ ☐   **8.** $7 + 2 =$ ☐   **9.** $6 + 2 =$ ☐

Find the total number of toys.

10. 7 horns in the box

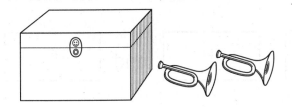

☐ Total

11. 5 bears in the box

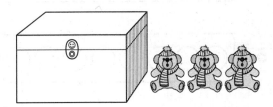

☐ Total

12. 3 balls in the box

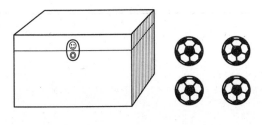

☐ Total

13. 8 train cars in the box

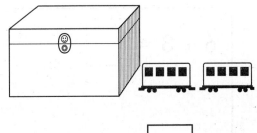

☐ Total

Remembering

1. Fill in the numbers from 0–10.

	1		4		6	7		

Show the 10-partners and switch the partners.

2. ○○○○○○○○○○　　 ☐ + 　and　 ☐ +

3. ○○○○○○○○○○　　 ☐ + 　and　 ☐ +

4. ○○○○○○○○○○　　 ☐ + 　and　 ☐ +

5. ○○○○○○○○○○　　 ☐ + 　and　 ☐ +

6. ○○○○○○○○○○　　 ☐ + 　and　 ☐ +

7. Stretch Your Thinking Count on with dots
to find the total. Write the total.

$6 + 3 = $ ☐

Addition Strategies: Counting On

Homework

Underline the greater number.
Count on from that number.

1. ● ● ●
3 + <u>6</u> = ☐

2. 2 + 5 = ☐

3. 2 + 8 = ☐

4. 7 + 3 = ☐

5. 4 + 5 = ☐

6. 3 + 5 = ☐

7. 2 + 7 = ☐

8. 6 + 4 = ☐

9. 4 + 3 = ☐

10. 2 + 6 = ☐

11. 8 + 2 = ☐

12. 6 + 3 = ☐

Remembering

Write the partners and the total.

1.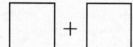

Total ☐

2.

Total ☐

3.

Total ☐

4.

Total ☐

Use patterns to solve.

5. $8 - 1 =$ ☐ $4 - 1 =$ ☐ $10 - 1 =$ ☐

6. $0 + 5 =$ ☐ $0 + 9 =$ ☐ $7 + 0 =$ ☐

7. $10 - 0 =$ ☐ $5 - 0 =$ ☐ $6 - 0 =$ ☐

8. Stretch Your Thinking Sami counts on to solve this problem. $2 + 8 =$ ☐
Sami counts 8, 9 and says the total is 9. What did she do wrong?

Homework

Underline the greater number.
Count on from that number.

1. $2 + \underline{7} =$ ☐

2. $1 + 9 =$ ☐

3. $3 + 4 =$ ☐

4. $6 + 3 =$ ☐

5. $4 + 5 =$ ☐

6. $3 + 7 =$ ☐

7. $2 + 4 =$ ☐

8. $5 + 3 =$ ☐

9. $8 + 2 =$ ☐

10. $5 + 2 =$ ☐

11. $3 + 6 =$ ☐

12. $6 + 2 =$ ☐

13. $2 + 8 =$ ☐

14. $7 + 3 =$ ☐

Remembering

Write the partners and the total.

1.  [ ] + [ ]

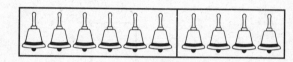

Total [ ]

2. 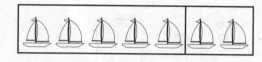 [ ] + [ ]

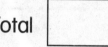

Total [ ]

3. [ ] + [ ]

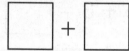

Total [ ]

4. [ ] + [ ]

Total [ ]

Write the partners and total for each circle drawing.

5. [ ] + [ ]

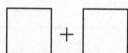

Total [ ]

6. [ ] + [ ]

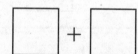

Total [ ]

7. Stretch Your Thinking Ring the greater number and count on from that number. Write the total.

$4 + 5 =$ [ ]

Addition Game: Unknown Totals

Homework

Underline the greater number.
Count on from that number.

1. ●●●●
$4 + \underline{5} = \square$

2. $6 + 3 = \square$

3. $3 + 5 = \square$

4. $2 + 3 = \square$

5. $2 + 8 = \square$

6. $4 + 2 = \square$

7. $4 + 3 = \square$

8. $7 + 3 = \square$

9. $8 + 2 = \square$

10. $6 + 2 = \square$

11. $3 + 7 = \square$

12. $5 + 2 = \square$

13. $2 + 7 = \square$

14. $7 + 2 = \square$

Remembering

Write the partners and total for each circle drawing.

1.

2.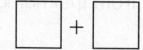

Total ☐

Total ☐

3.

4.

Total ☐

Total ☐

Write the partners and the total. Then write the equation.

5.

Total ☐

_____

Equation

6. **Stretch Your Thinking** Write an addition equation. Draw dots to count on to solve it.

Homework

Solve. Write how many are left.

1. There are 7 boats.

Then 4 sail away.

$7 - 4 =$

2. There are 10 candles.

Then 7 go out.

$10 - 7 =$

3. There are 8 muffins.

Then 6 are eaten.

$8 - 6 =$

4. There are 9 fish.

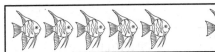

Then 5 swim away.

$9 - 5 =$

5. There are 6 elephants.

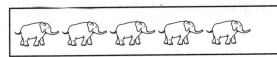

Then 4 go away.

$6 - 4 =$

Name _____

Remembering

Write the partners and the total. Then write the equation.

1.

Total ⬚

_____
Equation

2.

Total ⬚

_____
Equation

3.

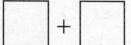

Total ⬚

_____
Equation

4. **Stretch Your Thinking** Write an equation
for this story problem. There are 8 ants.
Then 2 crawl away.

_____
Equation

Represent Subtraction

Name _____

Homework

Use the picture to solve the equation.

1.

$10 - 7 =$ ▢

2.

$7 - 2 =$ ▢

3.

$9 - 6 =$ ▢

4.

$8 - 4 =$ ▢

5.

$5 - 3 =$ ▢

6.

$6 - 2 =$ ▢

7.

$7 - 4 =$ ▢

8.

$9 - 4 =$ ▢

9.

$6 - 4 =$ ▢

10.

$8 - 5 =$ ▢

11.

$10 - 8 =$ ▢

12.

$7 - 7 =$ ▢

Name _____

Remembering

Count on. Write the total.

1. Total

 = ☐

2. Total

 = ☐

3. Total

2 🍓🍓🍓🍓🍓 = ☐

4. Total

4 🍆🍆 = ☐

Find the total number of toys.

5. 8 horns in the box

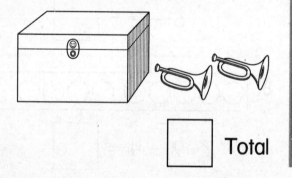

☐ Total

6. 7 train cars in the box

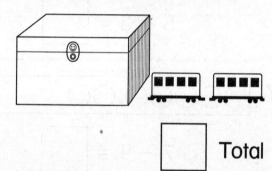

☐ Total

7. Stretch Your Thinking Make a circle drawing to show subtraction. Then write the equation.

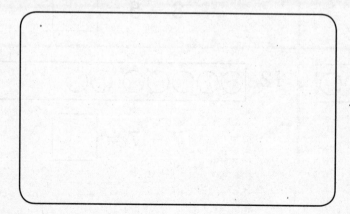

_____
Equation

Practice with Subtraction

Homework

Use the circles to solve the equation.

1. ○○○○○ ○○○○

$9 - 5 =$ ☐

2. ○○○○○ ○

$6 - 2 =$ ☐

3. ○○○○○ ○○○○○

$10 - 8 =$ ☐

4. ○○○○○ ○○○

$8 - 5 =$ ☐

5. ○○○○○ ○

$6 - 3 =$ ☐

6. ○○○○○

$5 - 2 =$ ☐

7. ○○○○○ ○○

$7 - 3 =$ ☐

8. ○○○○○ ○○○○

$9 - 6 =$ ☐

Solve the equation.

9. $6 - 4 =$ ☐

10. $8 - 6 =$ ☐

11. $10 - 2 =$ ☐

12. $7 - 1 =$ ☐

13. $9 - 7 =$ ☐

14. $8 - 1 =$ ☐

Name _____

Remembering

Find the total number of toys.

1. 4 balls in the box

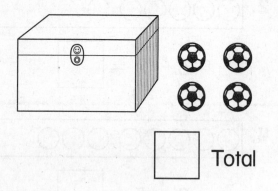

☐ Total

2. 6 bears in the box

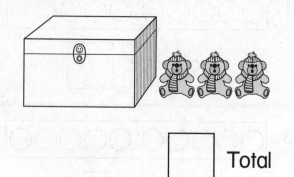

☐ Total

Underline the greater number.
Count on from that number.

3. $\underline{6} + 3 =$ ☐

4. $2 + 5 =$ ☐

5. $2 + 6 =$ ☐

6. $7 + 2 =$ ☐

7. $3 + 7 =$ ☐

8. $3 + 5 =$ ☐

9. Stretch Your Thinking Use a circle drawing
to solve this equation. Show your work.

$$8 - 5 = 3$$

Generate Subtraction Problems

Homework

Use addition to solve subtraction.

1. $5 + 5 = 10$, so I know $10 - 5 = \boxed{}$.

2. $6 + 4 = 10$, so I know $10 - 4 = \boxed{}$.

3. $3 + 6 = 9$, so I know $9 - 3 = \boxed{}$.

Solve the vertical form. Use any method.

4. $\begin{array}{r} 2 \\ +\,5 \\ \hline \end{array}$ **5.** $\begin{array}{r} 4 \\ +\,5 \\ \hline \end{array}$ **6.** $\begin{array}{r} 7 \\ +\,1 \\ \hline \end{array}$ **7.** $\begin{array}{r} 2 \\ +\,8 \\ \hline \end{array}$ **8.** $\begin{array}{r} 4 \\ +\,3 \\ \hline \end{array}$

9. $\begin{array}{r} 3 \\ +\,5 \\ \hline \end{array}$ **10.** $\begin{array}{r} 8 \\ +\,1 \\ \hline \end{array}$ **11.** $\begin{array}{r} 1 \\ +\,9 \\ \hline \end{array}$ **12.** $\begin{array}{r} 6 \\ +\,3 \\ \hline \end{array}$ **13.** $\begin{array}{r} 5 \\ +\,4 \\ \hline \end{array}$

Solve the vertical form. Think about addition.

14. $\begin{array}{r} 10 \\ -\,9 \\ \hline \end{array}$ **15.** $\begin{array}{r} 8 \\ -\,6 \\ \hline \end{array}$ **16.** $\begin{array}{r} 9 \\ -\,1 \\ \hline \end{array}$ **17.** $\begin{array}{r} 7 \\ -\,2 \\ \hline \end{array}$ **18.** $\begin{array}{r} 10 \\ -\,3 \\ \hline \end{array}$

19. $\begin{array}{r} 9 \\ -\,7 \\ \hline \end{array}$ **20.** $\begin{array}{r} 8 \\ -\,1 \\ \hline \end{array}$ **21.** $\begin{array}{r} 7 \\ -\,4 \\ \hline \end{array}$ **22.** $\begin{array}{r} 8 \\ -\,3 \\ \hline \end{array}$ **23.** $\begin{array}{r} 9 \\ -\,6 \\ \hline \end{array}$

Remembering

Underline the greater number.
Count on from that number.

1. 3 + <u>7</u> = ☐

2. 6 + 2 = ☐

3. 2 + 5 = ☐

4. 5 + 4 = ☐

5. 6 + 3 = ☐

6. 2 + 8 = ☐

7. 9 + 1 = ☐

8. 4 + 3 = ☐

9. 2 + 6 = ☐

10. 7 + 2 = ☐

11. 3 + 4 = ☐

12. 5 + 3 = ☐

13. 4 + 6 = ☐

14. 1 + 7 = ☐

15. Stretch Your Thinking Write the addition you
can use to solve the subtraction. Then solve.

10 − 3 = ☐   ☐ + ☐ = ☐

© Houghton Mifflin Harcourt Publishing Company

Relate Addition and Subtraction

Homework

Count on to add.

1. $4 + 2 =$ ☐ **2.** $3 + 5 =$ ☐ **3.** $6 + 2 =$ ☐

4. $\begin{array}{r} 6 \\ + 3 \\ \hline \end{array}$ • • • **5.** $\begin{array}{r} 5 \\ + 5 \\ \hline \end{array}$ **6.** $\begin{array}{r} 2 \\ + 7 \\ \hline \end{array}$ **7.** $\begin{array}{r} 3 \\ + 4 \\ \hline \end{array}$ **8.** $\begin{array}{r} 4 \\ + 4 \\ \hline \end{array}$

Subtract. Make a circle drawing if you wish.

9. $9 - 2 =$ ☐ **10.** $7 - 5 =$ ☐ **11.** $6 - 3 =$ ☐

12. $\begin{array}{r} 6 \\ - 2 \\ \hline \end{array}$ **13.** $\begin{array}{r} 9 \\ - 5 \\ \hline \end{array}$ **14.** $\begin{array}{r} 10 \\ - 7 \\ \hline \end{array}$ **15.** $\begin{array}{r} 5 \\ - 4 \\ \hline \end{array}$ **16.** $\begin{array}{r} 8 \\ - 2 \\ \hline \end{array}$

Mixed Practice with Equations **47**

Remembering

Solve. Write how many are left.

1. There are 9 candles.

$$9 - 7 = \boxed{}$$

Then 7 go out.

---

2. There are 8 boats.

$$8 - 4 = \boxed{}$$

Then 4 sail away.

Subtract and write the equation.

3. ⭕⭕⭕⭕⭕ ⭕⭕⭕⭕⭕

Subtract 4   _____

               Equation

---

4. ⭕⭕⭕⭕⭕ ⭕⭕

Subtract 2   _____

               Equation

---

5. Stretch Your Thinking Write numbers to complete the subtraction.

$$\boxed{} - \boxed{} = 5$$

      Mixed Practice with Equations

Homework

Draw a picture to show the story.
Write and solve the equation.

Karl sees 2 owls and 5 eagles in a park.

How many birds does he see?

$2 + 5 = \boxed{}$

Focus on Mathematical Practices **49**

Name

Remembering

Use the circles to solve the equation.

1. ⬭ ◯◯◯◯◯ ◯◯◯◯◯ ⬭

$$10 - 4 = \boxed{}$$

2. ⬭ ◯◯◯◯◯ ◯◯◯◯ ⬭

$$9 - 2 = \boxed{}$$

Use addition to solve subtraction.

3. $7 + 3 = 10$, so I know $10 - 3 = \boxed{}$.

4. $9 + 1 = 10$, so I know $10 - 1 = \boxed{}$.

5. $4 + 5 = \boxed{}$, so I know $9 - 4 = \boxed{}$.

Solve the vertical form. Think about addition.

6. $\begin{array}{r} 6 \\ -1 \\ \hline \end{array}$ **7.** $\begin{array}{r} 8 \\ -4 \\ \hline \end{array}$ **8.** $\begin{array}{r} 9 \\ -7 \\ \hline \end{array}$ **9.** $\begin{array}{r} 10 \\ -3 \\ \hline \end{array}$ **10.** $\begin{array}{r} 7 \\ -6 \\ \hline \end{array}$

11. Stretch Your Thinking

Solve.

If I know $7 - 4 = \boxed{}$,

then I know $\boxed{} + \boxed{} = \boxed{}$.

Focus on Mathematical Practices

Homework

Solve the story problem.

Show your work. Use drawings, numbers, or words.

---

1. I see 8 bees in the sky.

5 fly low. The others fly high.

How many bees fly high?

bee

[ ] _____

label

---

2. 7 cars are in the parking lot.

Then more cars come.

Now there are 9.

How many more cars come?

parking lot

[ ] _____

label

Find the unknown partner.

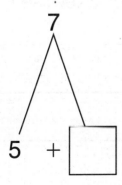

3. 7 → 5 + [ ]

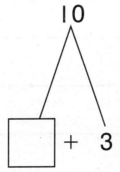

4. 10 → [ ] + 3

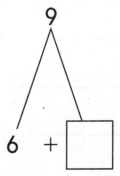

5. 9 → 6 + [ ]

Remembering

Show and write the 6-partners.

1.

○ ○ ○ ○ ○ ○	+	$6 = 5 + 1$
○ ○ ○ ○ ○ ○	+	$6 =$ _____
○ ○ ○ ○ ○ ○	+	$6 =$ _____
○ ○ ○ ○ ○ ○	+	$6 =$ _____
○ ○ ○ ○ ○ ○	+	$6 =$ _____

Find the unknown partner.

2. 8
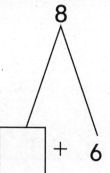
□ + 6

3. 7
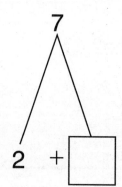
2 + □

4. 10
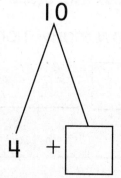
4 + □

5. Stretch Your Thinking Write a story problem for Exercise 4.

_____

_____

_____

_____

Problems with Unknown Partners

Name _____

Homework

Count on to find the unknown partner.

1. $3 + \boxed{} = 7$ 2. $5 + \boxed{} = 10$ 3. $2 + \boxed{} = 6$

4. $4 + \boxed{} = 8$ 5. $7 + \boxed{} = 9$ 6. $5 + \boxed{} = 9$

7. $6 + \boxed{} = 9$ $4 + \boxed{} = 10$ 9. $4 + \boxed{} = 7$

Count on to find the number of animals in the barn.

10. 8 total

$\boxed{}$ in the barn

1. 9 total

$\boxed{}$ in the barn

12. 10 total

$\boxed{}$ in the barn

13. 7 total

$\boxed{}$ in the barn

Name _____

Remembering

Write the partners and the switched partners.

1.

7-train

Count on. Write the total.

2.

Total

7 🍓🍓🍓 = ☐

3.

5 🍎🍎 = ☐

Total

4.

2 🍑🍑🍑🍑 = ☐

Total

5.

8 🎃 = ☐

Total

Show your work. Use drawings, numbers, or words.

Solve the story problem.

6. Ben sees 9 ducks in the pond.
   3 are white. The others are black.
   How many ducks are black?

   ☐ _____
        label

duck

7. **Stretch Your Thinking** Write three
   addition equations with a total of 10.

   _____

Solve Equations with Unknown Partners

Homework

Count on to find the unknown partner.

1. $6 + \boxed{} = 9$ **2.** $5 + \boxed{} = 7$ **3.** $8 + \boxed{} = 9$

4. $3 + \boxed{} = 8$ **5.** $7 + \boxed{} = 10$ **6.** $4 + \boxed{} = 8$

Solve the story problem.

Show your work. Use drawings, numbers or words.

---

7. We make 10 pumpkin pies today.

6 pies are hot.

The rest are cold.

How many pies are cold?

$\boxed{}$ _____
      label

pumpkin

---

8. I have 4 kites.

Then I buy more.

Now I have 7 kites.

How many kites do I buy?

$\boxed{}$ _____
      label

kite

© Houghton Mifflin Harcourt Publishing Company

Remembering

Show the 8-partners and switch the partners.

1.

Add.

2. $2 + 5 = \boxed{}$ **3.** $2 + 4 = \boxed{}$ **4.** $8 + 2 = \boxed{}$

5. $2 + 8 = \boxed{}$ **6.** $7 + 2 = \boxed{}$ **7.** $5 + 2 = \boxed{}$

Subtract.

8. $5 - 2 = \boxed{}$ **9.** $9 - 2 = \boxed{}$ **10.** $7 - 2 = \boxed{}$

11. $8 - 2 = \boxed{}$ **12.** $6 - 2 = \boxed{}$ **13.** $10 - 2 = \boxed{}$

14. Stretch Your Thinking Write an addition equation with 3 as the unknown partner.

Name _____

Homework

Count on to find the unknown partner.

1. $5 + \boxed{} = 7$ **2.** $3 + \boxed{} = 9$ **3.** $4 + \boxed{} = 7$

4. $4 + \boxed{} = 8$ **5.** $6 + \boxed{} = 10$ **6.** $5 + \boxed{} = 9$

Solve the story problem.

Show your work. Use drawings, numbers, or words.

farm

7. Amanda picks 2 melons
at the farm.

Rosa also picks some.

Together they pick 7 melons.

How many does Rosa pick?

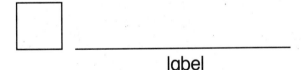

$\boxed{}$ _____
label

mask

8. I have 10 masks.

7 masks are black.

The others are white.

How many masks are white?

$\boxed{}$ _____
label

Remembering

Show the 9-partners and switch the partners.

1.
| ○○○○○○○○○ | ☐ + ☐ | and | ☐ + ☐ |

| ○○○○○○○○○ | ☐ + ☐ | and | ☐ + ☐ |

| ○○○○○○○○○ | ☐ + ☐ | and | ☐ + ☐ |

| ○○○○○○○○○ | ☐ + ☐ | and | ☐ + ☐ |

Underline the greater number.
Count on from that number.

2. $3 + 7 = $ ☐   **3.** $5 + 3 = $ ☐

4. $7 + 2 = $ ☐   **5.** $3 + 6 = $ ☐

Count on to find the unknown partner.

6. $3 + $ ☐ $ = 10$ **7.** $4 + $ ☐ $ = 6$ **8.** $2 + $ ☐ $ = 9$

9. $4 + $ ☐ $ = 7$ **10.** $3 + $ ☐ $ = 8$ **11.** $4 + $ ☐ $ = 10$

12. Stretch Your Thinking Sal has 6 balloons.
He buys some more. Then he has 10 balloons.
How many balloons does Sal buy?

_____ balloons

© Houghton Mifflin Harcourt Publishing Company

Practice with Unknown Partners

Homework

Count on to solve.

1. $6 - 4 = \boxed{}$ 2. $10 - 7 = \boxed{}$ 3. $8 - 3 = \boxed{}$

4. $\begin{array}{r} 9 \\ -5 \\ \hline \end{array}$ 5. $\begin{array}{r} 8 \\ -5 \\ \hline \end{array}$ 6. $\begin{array}{r} 7 \\ -3 \\ \hline \end{array}$

Solve the story problem.

Show your work. Use drawings, numbers, or words.

---

7. 6 bowls are on a tray.
   We take 3 away.
   How many bowls are left?

tray

$\boxed{}$ _____
          label

---

8. I see 10 bugs on the step.
   6 of them fly away.
   How many bugs are still there?

bug

$\boxed{}$ _____
          label

Remembering

Write the 10-partners and the switched partners.

1.
●●●●●   ●●●●●   ●●●●●   ●●●●●   ●●●●●
●●●●○   ●●●○○   ●●○○○   ●○○○○   ○○○○○

$\underline{9 + 1}$ $\underline{+}$ $\underline{+}$ $\underline{+}$ $\underline{+}$

$\underline{1 + 9}$ $\underline{+}$ $\underline{+}$ $\underline{+}$ $\underline{+}$

Underline the greater number.
Count on from that number.

2. $5 + 2 =$ ▢

3. $8 + 2 =$ ▢

4. $3 + 5 =$ ▢

5. $3 + 7 =$ ▢

Show your work. Use drawings, numbers, or words.

Solve the story problem.

6. Kate has 2 books. She buys some more. Then she has 9 books. How many books does Kate buy?

book

▢ _____
     label

7. **Stretch Your Thinking** Look at the story problem above. Does the answer need a label to make sense? Explain.

_____

_____

Homework

Count on to solve.

1. $8 - 4 =$ ☐　　　**2.** $10 - 6 =$ ☐　　　**3.** $7 - 5 =$ ☐

4.　　9
　　　$- 4$
　　　‾‾‾

5.　　5
　　　$- 3$
　　　‾‾‾

6.　　7
　　　$- 2$
　　　‾‾‾

Solve the story problem.

Show your work. Use drawings, numbers, or words.

7. 10 people are on the bus. Then 7 of them get off. How many people are on the bus now?

bus

☐ _____
　　label

8. Dan has 10 shells in his bag. Then he gives away 3 shells. How many shells does he have now?

shell

☐ _____
　　label

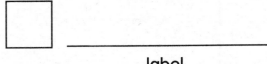

Remembering

Subtract.

1. 8 − 1 = ☐   **2.** 3 − 1 = ☐   **3.** 10 − 1 = ☐

4. 7 − 0 = ☐   **5.** 4 − 0 = ☐   **6.** 9 − 0 = ☐

Use doubles to solve.

7. 2 + 2 = ☐   **8.** 5 + 5 = ☐   **9.** 4 + 4 = ☐

10. 4 − 2 = ☐   **11.** 10 − 5 = ☐   **12.** 8 − 4 = ☐

Solve the story problem.

Show your work. Use drawings, numbers, or words.

13. I have 10 buttons. 8 are black. The others are red. How many buttons are red?

button

☐ _____
     label

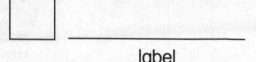

14. Stretch Your Thinking Draw a Math Mountain to solve Problem 13.

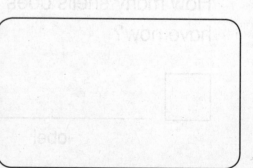

Homework

Count on to solve.

1. $6 - 4 = \boxed{}$ 2. $9 - 5 = \boxed{}$ 3. $8 - 2 = \boxed{}$

4. $\begin{array}{r} 10 \\ - \\ \hline \end{array}$ 5. $\begin{array}{r} 7 \\ -3 \\ \hline \end{array}$ 6. $\begin{array}{r} 9 \\ -6 \\ \hline \end{array}$

Solve the story problem.

Show your work. Use drawings, numbers, or words.

swing

7. 7 girls are playing. 3 are jumping rope. The rest are on the swings. How many girls are on the swings?

$\boxed{}$ _____
label

bat

8. I see 9 bats in a tree. Then 2 of them fly away. How many bats are left?

$\boxed{}$ _____
label

Remembering

Underline the greater number.
Count on from that number.

1. $3 + 6 =$ ▢

2. $3 + 2 =$ ▢

3. $5 + 2 =$ ▢

4. $2 + 8 =$ ▢

Count on to solve.

5. $8 - 5 =$ ▢

6. $7 - 3 =$ ▢

7. $10 - 8 =$ ▢

8. $\begin{array}{r} 7 \\ -4 \\ \hline \end{array}$

9. $\begin{array}{r} 6 \\ -4 \\ \hline \end{array}$

10. $\begin{array}{r} 9 \\ -5 \\ \hline \end{array}$

Solve the story problem.

Show your work. Use drawings, numbers, or words.

11. 9 children are playing tag.
Then 6 children are out.
How many children are
playing tag now?

children

▢ _____
label

12. Stretch Your Thinking Write an equation
for Problem 11.

_____

Practice with Subtraction Stories

Homework

Name _____

Solve. Watch the signs.

1. $3 + 7 = \boxed{}$ 2. $6 + \boxed{} = 9$ 3. $\boxed{} + 2 = 7$

4. $7 - 2 = \boxed{}$ 5. $8 - \boxed{} = 4$ 6. $\boxed{} - 2 = 8$

Solve the story problem.

Show your work. Use drawings, numbers, or words.

7. I see 8 clouds in the sky.
   Then 6 clouds float away.
   How many clouds are left?

   $\boxed{}$ _____
   label

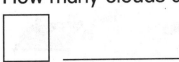
cloud

8. We see 5 butterflies on the fence. Then
   some land on a rock. Now there are 9
   butterflies. How many land on the rock?

   $\boxed{}$ _____
   label

fence

9. Some boats are at the dock. Then 4 sail
   away. Now there are 6 boats. How many
   boats were there before?

   $\boxed{}$ _____
   label

boat

© Houghton Mifflin Harcourt Publishing Company

Remembering

Subtract and write the equation.

1.
   _____
   Subtract 4   Equation

2.
   _____
   Subtract 5   Equation

Find the number of animals in the barn.

3. 8 total

☐ in the barn

4. 10 total

☐ in the barn

Solve. Watch the signs.

5. $5 + 4 =$ ☐   6. $7 +$ ☐ $= 10$ 7. ☐ $+ 2 = 10$

8. $8 - 4 =$ ☐   9. $7 -$ ☐ $= 4$ 10. ☐ $- 2 = 4$

11. **Stretch Your Thinking** How did you solve Exercise 6.

_____

_____

      Solve Mixed Problems

Name _____

Homework

Solve. Watch the signs.

1. $3 + 6 = \boxed{}$

2. $5 + \boxed{} = 9$

3. $\boxed{} + 2 = 7$

4. $7 - 4 = \boxed{}$

5. $10 - \boxed{} = 7$

6. $\boxed{} - 5 = 3$

Solve the story problem.

Show your work. Use drawings, numbers, or words.

7. We see some zebras. 6 of them leave. Now there are 2 zebras. How many zebras are there at first?

zebra

$\boxed{}$ _____
label

8. Tim had 10 toy cars in his room. Then he gives some away. Now there are 4. How many toy cars does he give away?

toy car

$\boxed{}$ _____
label

9. Zoe has 4 pencils in her desk. She gets some more pencils. Now she has 9 pencils. How many pencils does she get?

desk

$\boxed{}$ _____
label

Practice with Mixed Problems **71**

Remembering

Add.

1. 8
    + 2

2. 3
    + 7

3. 1
    + 9

4. 6
    + 4

5. 5
    + 5

6. 4
    + 6

Count on to find the unknown partner.

7. 8 + ☐ = 10   **8.** 2 + ☐ = 7   **9.** 9 + ☐ = 10

10. 5 + ☐ = 7   **11.** 7 + ☐ = 10   **12.** 4 + ☐ = 8

Solve the story problem.   **Show your work. Use drawings,
                                             numbers, or words.**

13. I see 9 cars in the lot. Then
    4 cars drive away. How many
    cars are left?
                                             car

    ☐ _____
         label

14. **Stretch Your Thinking** Sal writes the equation

    4 + ☐5☐ = 9 to solve Problem 13.

    Write a subtraction equation to solve the problem.

    _____

Homework

Use the picture to write a story problem.
Write and solve the equation.

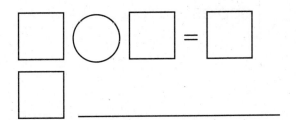

label

Name _____

Remembering

Solve the story problem.

Show your work. Use drawings, numbers, or words.

1. Yolanda has 9 cats. 2 are black. The others are white. How many cats are white?

   cat

   ▢ _____
   label

2. 5 lemons are on a tray. We take away 3. How many lemons are left?

   tray

   ▢ _____
   label

3. I have 8 CDs. I buy some more CDs. Now I have 10 CDs. How many CDs do I buy?

   CD

   ▢ _____
   label

4. **Stretch Your Thinking** Fill in the numbers to make your own problem. Then solve.

   I have ▢ apples.

   I buy some more. Now I have ▢ apples.

   How many apples do I buy?

   ▢ _____
   label

Focus on Mathematical Practices

Name _____

Homework

How many stars? Count by tens.

1.

_____ _____ _____ _____ _____ _____ _____   **Total**

Add 1 ten.

2.

$$60 + 10 = \boxed{}$$

3.

$$20 + 10 = \boxed{}$$

---

4. $80 + 10 = \boxed{}$ **5.** $90 + 10 = \boxed{}$

6. $40 + 10 = \boxed{}$ **7.** $70 + 10 = \boxed{}$

Introduction to Tens Groupings **75**

Remembering

Write the partners.

1.

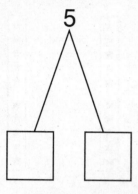　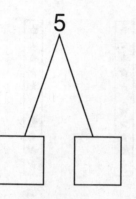　

Write the partners and total for each circle drawing.

2. ☐ + ☐

● ● ● ● ● ● | ○ ○ ○ ○ ○

Total ☐

3. ☐ + ☐

● ● ● ● ● | ● ● | ○ ○

Total ☐

Solve the story problem.

Show your work. Use drawings, numbers, or words.

4. 5 chicks are in the coop. Some more chicks join them. Now there are 9 chicks. How many chicks join?

chick

☐ _____
　　　label

5. **Stretch Your Thinking** What number is 5 tens and 10 ones? Write the number. Draw to explain.

☐　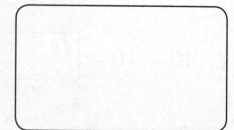

Introduction to Tens Groupings

Homework

Name _____

Write how many.

1.

2.

3.

4.

5.

Find the unknown total or partner.

6. $10 + 6 =$ ☐

7. $10 +$ ☐ $= 18$

8. $10 + 1 =$ ☐

9. $10 +$ ☐ $= 15$

Start at 10. Count. Write the teen numbers.

10. | 10 | | | | 14 |

| | | 17 | | |

Remembering

Write the partners and the switched partners.

1.
8-train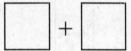

| + | + | + | + |
| + | + | + | + |

Write the partners and the total. Then write the equation.

2. ☐ + ☐

_____
Equation

Total ☐

Add 1 ten.

3. 60 + 10 = ☐   4. 20 + 10 = ☐

5. 80 + 10 = ☐   6. 50 + 10 = ☐

7. 70 + 10 = ☐   8. 30 + 10 = ☐

9. **Stretch Your Thinking** If 10 + 7 = 17,
then what is 20 + 7? Draw to explain.

20 + 7 = ☐

Name

Homework

Write how many.

1.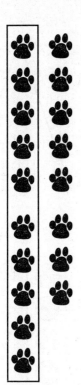

2.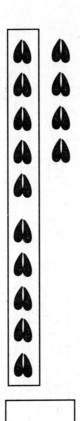

3.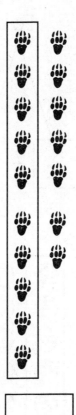

4.

Find the total.

5. $10 + 9 =$

6. $10 + 4 =$

7. $10 + 2 =$

8. $10 + 8 =$

9. $10 + 6 =$

Write the teen number.

10. ○ ○ ○ ○ ○

11. ○ ○ ○ ○ ○
○ ○ ○ ○

12. ○ ○ ○ ○ ○
○ ○

Name _____

Remembering

Find the unknown partner.

1. 10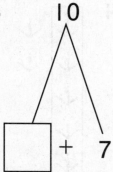
☐ + 7

2. 9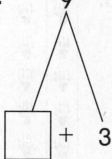
☐ + 3

3. 8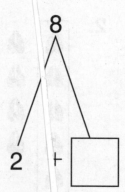
2 + ☐

4. 7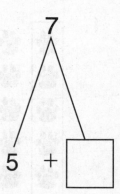
5 + ☐

Write how many.

5.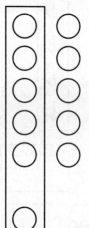

6.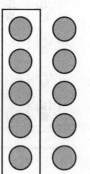

7.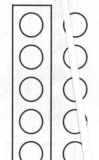

8.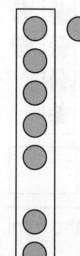

9. Stretch Your Thinking Write or
draw two different ways to
show the number 13.

Represent and Compare Teen Numbers

Homework

Name _____

Solve the story problem.

Show your work. Use drawings, numbers, or words.

1. There are 5 boys inside the tent and 8 boys outside the tent. How many boys are there?

tent

[   ] _____

label

2. I caught 9 fish yesterday. I catch 7 fish today. How many fish do I catch in all?

fish

[   ] _____

label

Find the teen total.

3. $8 + 7 =$ [   ]   **4.** $9 + 3 =$ [   ]   **5.** $4 + 8 =$ [   ]

6. $9 + 6 =$ [   ]   **7.** $8 + 8 =$ [   ]   **8.** $8 + 9 =$ [   ]

9. $7 + 7 =$ [   ]   **10.** $5 + 7 =$ [   ]   **11.** $6 + 5 =$ [   ]

Remembering

Count on to find the total.

1. $2 + 5 = \boxed{}$ **2.** $4 + 2 = \boxed{}$ **3.** $3 + 7 = \boxed{}$

4. $6 + 4 = \boxed{}$ **5.** $3 + 5 = \boxed{}$ **6.** $5 + 4 = \boxed{}$

Count on to find the unknown partner.

7. $6 + \boxed{} = 9$ **8.** $8 + \boxed{} = 10$ **9.** $5 + \boxed{} = 10$

10. $5 + \boxed{} = 8$ **11.** $4 + \boxed{} = 7$ **12.** $7 + \boxed{} = 9$

Write an equation for the drawing. Then make a ten.

13. 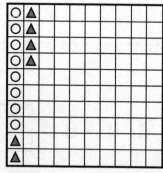   **14.** 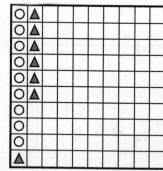   **15.**

_____   _____   _____

_____   _____   _____

16. Stretch Your Thinking Write a story

problem for $9 + 5 = \boxed{}$. Solve it.

_____

_____

Teen Addition Strategies

Homework

Name _____

Find the total.

1. $9 + 9 =$ ☐   **2.** $5 + 5 =$ ☐   **3.** $8 + 8 =$ ☐

4. $7 + 7 =$ ☐   **5.** $10 + 10 =$ ☐   **6.** $6 + 6 =$ ☐

Use a double to find the total.

7. $6 + 8 =$ ☐   **8.** $8 + 9 =$ ☐   **9.** $7 + 6 =$ ☐

10. $5 + 6 =$ ☐   **11.** $7 + 9 =$ ☐   **12.** $5 + 4 =$ ☐

13. $7 + 5 =$ ☐   **14.** $7 + 8 =$ ☐   **15.** $6 + 4 =$ ☐

16. $9 + 8 =$ ☐   **17.** $8 + 7 =$ ☐   **18.** $8 + 10 =$ ☐

19. $8 + 6 =$ ☐   **20.** $6 + 5 =$ ☐   **21.** $9 + 10 =$ ☐

22. $6 + 7 =$ ☐   **23.** $9 + 7 =$ ☐   **24.** $5 + 7 =$ ☐

Name _____

Remembering

Underline the greater number.
Count on from that number.

1. $2 + 8 =$ ☐

2. $7 + 3 =$ ☐

3. $5 + 2 =$ ☐

4. $4 + 5 =$ ☐

Solve the story problem.

Show your work. Use drawings, numbers, or words.

5. Adam has 10 apples. 7 apples are
   red and the rest are green.
   How many apples are green?

apple

☐ _____
  label

6. I read 8 books this week. I read
   7 books last week. How many
   books do I read in all?

book

☐ _____
  label

7. **Stretch Your Thinking** Look for a pattern.
   Find the double of 11.

$$8 + 8 = 16$$
$$9 + 9 = 18$$
$$10 + 10 = 20$$
$$11 + 11 = \boxed{}$$

Investigate Doubles

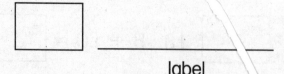

Homework

1. How many turtles?

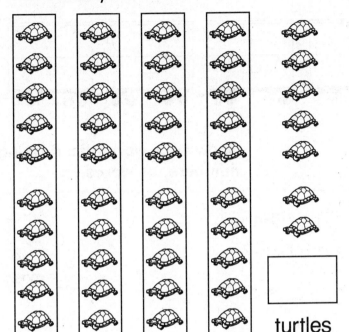

turtles

2. How many butterflies?

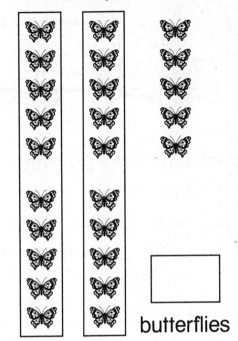

butterflies

Write the numbers.

3.

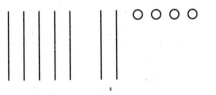

_____ = _____ tens _____ ones

4.

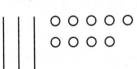

_____ = _____ tens _____ ones

5.

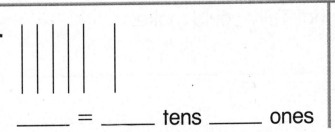

_____ = _____ tens _____ ones

Draw 10-sticks and circles.

6. 52

7. 26

8. 48

Name _____

Remembering

Write the partners and the switched partners.

1.

10-train

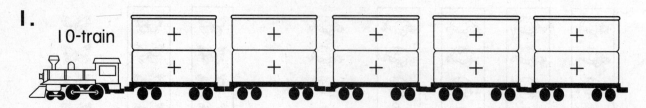

Solve the story problem.

Show your work. Use drawings, numbers, or words.

2. I have 9 masks. 4 are red. The others are blue. How many masks are blue?

☐ _____
label

mask

Use a double to find the total.

3. 6 + 5 = ☐

4. 9 + 8 = ☐

5. 7 + 6 = ☐

6. 5 + 7 = ☐

7. 7 + 9 = ☐

8. 6 + 8 = ☐

9. Stretch Your Thinking Tully draws four 10-sticks and less than ten circles to make a number. Write the numbers that Tully could make.

_____

_____

Understand Tens and Ones

Write the numbers.

1.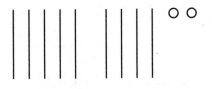

_____ = _____ tens _____ ones

2.

||||| |||| ○ ○

_____ = _____ tens _____ ones

Draw 10-sticks and circles.

3. 81

4. 27

Write the number. Ring the number word.

5. ||

[ ] two   twelve   twenty

6.

[ ] one   ten   eleven

7. |||||

[ ] four   fourteen   forty

8.

[ ] three   thirteen   thirty

Remembering

Underline the greater number.
Count on from that number.

1. $5 + 2 =$ ▢

2. $6 + 3 =$ ▢

3. $3 + 7 =$ ▢

4. $1 + 9 =$ ▢

Write the number.

5. ||||| ○○○○○ ○○ ▢

6. ||||| | ○○○○ ▢

Draw 10-sticks and circles.

7. 82

8. 39

Solve the story problem.

Show your work. Use drawings, numbers, or words.

9. Aria has 10 dolls. She gives 5 of them away. How many dolls are left?

▢ _____
     label

doll

10. Stretch Your Thinking Sue says the drawing shows 35. Liam says the drawing shows 53. Ring the tens. Underline the ones. Write the correct number.

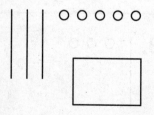

Integrate Tens and Ones

Name _____

Homework

Write the number.

1. ||||| | ○ ○ [   ]

2. | ○ ○ ○ ○ ○
     ○ ○   [   ]

Draw 10-sticks and circles.

3. 73

4. 19

Draw 10-sticks and circles. Write the number shown.

5. [   ] = 30 + 4

6. [   ] = 50 + 6

7. [   ] = 40 + 1

8. [   ] = 60 + 5

Write the next number.

9. | 38 | 39 | [   ] |

10. | 58 | 59 | [   ] |

11. | 88 | 89 | [   ] |

12. | 48 | 49 | [   ] |

Remembering

Count on to solve.

1. $8 - 4 =$ ☐ 2. $10 - 7 =$ ☐ 3. $9 - 5 =$ ☐

4. 9
    $- 6$

5. 7
    $- 5$

6. 10
    $- 8$

Write the number. Ring the number word.

7. |||| ||| ☐   eight   eighteen   eighty

8. ○ ○ ○ ○ ○
   ○ ○   ☐   seven   seventeen   seventy

Find the total. Then make a ten.

9. $8 + 7 =$ ☐

   $10 +$ ☐ $=$ ☐

10. $5 + 9 =$ ☐

    $10 +$ ☐ $=$ ☐

11. **Stretch Your Thinking** What number is 1 more than 99? Draw to show how you know.

☐

☐

© Houghton Mifflin Harcourt Publishing Company

Practice Grouping Ones into Tens

Homework

Name _____

Each jar has 10 beans. How many beans are there?

1.

2.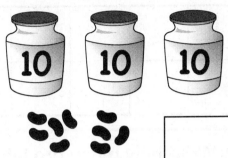

3.

4.

Each box in the bagel shop holds 10 bagels.
Draw to solve the story problem.

5. There are 7 boxes and
4 extra bagels. How
many bagels are there?

6. There are 3 boxes and
8 extra bagels. How
many bagels are there?

☐ bagels

☐ bagels

Name _____

Remembering

1. Write the numbers from 1–20.

1	2					7			
11			14						

Solve. Write how many are left.

2. There are 8 butterflies.

Then 5 fly away.

$8 - 5 = \boxed{}$

3. There are 10 turtles.

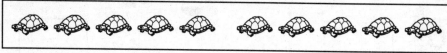

Then 8 crawl away.

$10 - 8 = \boxed{}$

Write the next number.

4.

78	79	

5.

48	49	

6.

88	89	

7.

68	69	

8. Stretch Your Thinking Choose and ring a way to solve 6 + 7. Then draw to show your work.

count on

make a ten

doubles plus 1

Add with Groups of Ten

Name _____

Homework

Each box has 10 crayons. How many crayons are there?

1.

2.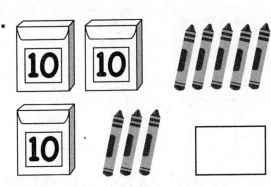

3.

4.

Write the numbers.

5.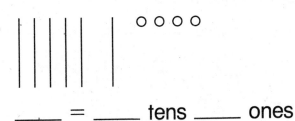

_____ = _____ tens _____ ones

6.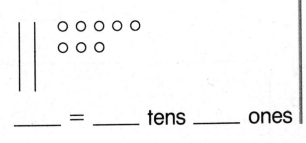

_____ = _____ tens _____ ones

Draw 10-sticks and circles.

7. 34

8. 62

Practice with Tens and Ones **95**

Remembering

1. Write how many dots. See the 5 in each group.

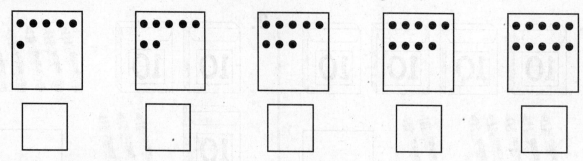

Solve the vertical form. Use any method.

2. 4 +5	**3.** 3 +7	**4.** 9 +1	**5.** 1 +9	**6.** 5 +2

7. 3 +3	**8.** 3 +5	**9.** 1 +8	**10.** 4 +6	**11.** 4 +4

Each jar has 10 beans. How many beans are there?

12.

13.

14. Stretch Your Thinking Draw a new problem like Exercise 13. Show groups of ten and extras. Write the number.

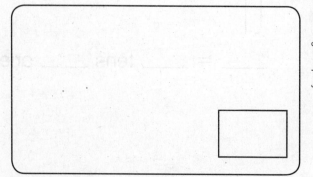

Practice with Tens and Ones

Homework

Compare the numbers.

Write >, <, or =.

1. ‖ ∘∘∘∘∘ ‖‖‖∘

25 ◯ 41

2. ‖‖ ∘∘∘∘∘ ∘∘ ‖‖‖ ∘∘

37 ◯ 32

3. 46 ◯ 46   **4.** 80 ◯ 79   **5.** 30 ◯ 40

6. 84 ◯ 93   **7.** 51 ◯ 37   **8.** 61 ◯ 16

9. 44 ◯ 4   **10.** 75 ◯ 75   **11.** 56 ◯ 57

Compare the numbers two ways.

Write the numbers.

12. Compare 18 and 21.

13. Compare 76 and 67.

14. Compare 42 and 43.

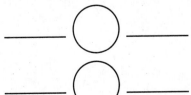

15. Compare 50 and 95.

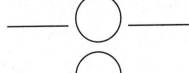

Remembering

Subtract and write the equation.

1. ⬜ ○○○○○ ○○○○○ ⬜ _____
Equation

Subtract 4

2. ⬜ ○○○○○ ○○○○○ ⬜ _____
Equation

Subtract 6

Solve. Watch the signs.

3. $5 + 5 = \boxed{}$ **4.** $8 + \boxed{} = 9$ **5.** $\boxed{} + 4 = 8$

6. $8 - 4 = \boxed{}$ **7.** $10 - \boxed{} = 7$ **8.** $\boxed{} - 2 = 7$

Write the number.

9. 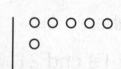   **10.**

11. Stretch Your Thinking Write a number that is greater than 55 and less than 65.

   Use Place Value to Compare Numbers

Homework

Add.

1. $4 + 2 =$ ☐ $40 + 20 =$ ☐

2. $3 + 5 =$ ☐ $30 + 50 =$ ☐

3. $6 + 3 =$ ☐ $60 + 30 =$ ☐

4. $2 + 5 =$ ☐ $20 + 50 =$ ☐

5. $50 + 1 =$ ☐ $50 + 10 =$ ☐

6. $80 + 1 =$ ☐ $80 + 10 =$ ☐

7. Each can has 10 peaches. How many
    peaches are there in all?

☐ peaches

Name _____

Remembering

Solve the story problem.   **Show your work. Use drawings, numbers, or words.**

1. Noah sees 10 turtles. Some turtles swim away. Now there are 4 turtles. How many turtles swim away?

turtle

[   ] _____
          label

Find the unknown partner.

2. $5 + \boxed{} = 6$ **3.** $8 + \boxed{} = 9$ **4.** $6 + \boxed{} = 10$

5. $8 + \boxed{} = 10$ **6.** $5 + \boxed{} = 8$ **7.** $2 + \boxed{} = 7$

Compare the numbers.
Write $<$, $>$, or $=$.

8. 28 $\bigcirc$ 28   **9.** 18 $\bigcirc$ 81   **10.** 34 $\bigcirc$ 36

11. 97 $\bigcirc$ 79   **12.** 53 $\bigcirc$ 53   **13.** 60 $\bigcirc$ 59

14. Stretch Your Thinking Choose a number between 25 and 37. Write your number. Add a ten. Then add another ten. Write the new number.

My Number   New Number

© Houghton Mifflin Harcourt Publishing Company

Add Tens or Ones

Homework

Find the total.

1. 38 + 4 = ☐   **2.** 42 + 5 = ☐   **3.** 56 + 7 = ☐

4. 78 + 2 = ☐   **5.** 60 + 8 = ☐   **6.** 15 + 4 = ☐

7. 59 + 3 = ☐   **8.** 92 + 6 = ☐   **9.** 81 + 5 = ☐

10. 12 + 5 = ☐   **11.** 23 + 7 = ☐   **12.** 64 + 7 = ☐

Count. Write the numbers.

13.

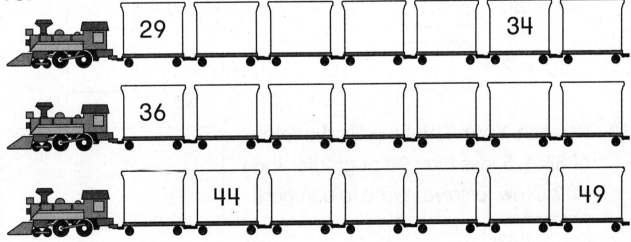

Remembering

Solve. Watch the signs.

1. $2 + 5 = \boxed{}$ 2. $6 + \boxed{} = 10$ 3. $\boxed{} + 8 = 10$

4. $9 - 4 = \boxed{}$ 5. $10 - \boxed{} = 1$ 6. $\boxed{} - 6 = 1$

Write the number.

7. | | | | | | | | | $\boxed{}$

8. | ° ° $\boxed{}$

Draw 10-sticks and circles.

9. 25

10. 58

Solve.

11. $5 + 2 = \boxed{}$

   $50 + 20 = \boxed{}$

   $50 + 2 = \boxed{}$

12. $8 + 1 = \boxed{}$

   $80 + 10 = \boxed{}$

   $80 + 1 = \boxed{}$

13. **Stretch Your Thinking** Is the total
of $86 + 5$ less than 90 or greater than
90? Draw to solve. Write to compare.

Counting On Strategy: 2-Digit Numbers

Homework

Count on to add.

1. $48 + 3 =$ ☐

2. $72 + 4 =$ ☐

3. $69 + 4 =$ ☐

4. $30 + 9 =$ ☐

5. $50 + 7 =$ ☐

6. $86 + 5 =$ ☐

7. $36 + 2 =$ ☐

8. $47 + 6 =$ ☐

9. $23 + 5 =$ ☐

10. $59 + 7 =$ ☐

11. ☐ $= 12 + 6$

12. ☐ $= 60 + 9$

13. ☐ $= 39 + 3$

14. ☐ $= 49 + 1$

15. ☐ $= 22 + 7$

16. ☐ $= 65 + 9$

Remembering

1. Write the numbers from 1–20.

Solve the story problem.

Show your work. Use drawings, numbers, or words.

2. Matt has 8 seeds to plant in a red pot and a blue pot. How many seeds can he plant in each pot? Show two answers.

seeds

[ ] seeds in the red pot and [ ] seeds in the blue pot

or [ ] seeds in the red pot and [ ] seeds in the blue pot

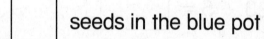

Find the total. Use any method.

3. 48 + 6 = [ ]   **4.** 39 + 4 = [ ]

5. 77 + 7 = [ ]   **6.** 85 + 9 = [ ]

7. Stretch Your Thinking Draw 10-sticks and circles to show the number that is 1 more than 89. Write the number.

[ ]

2-Digit Addition Games

© Houghton Mifflin Harcourt Publishing Company

Homework

Draw to show each number.

1. There are 20 boys and girls in a show.
   There are more girls than boys.

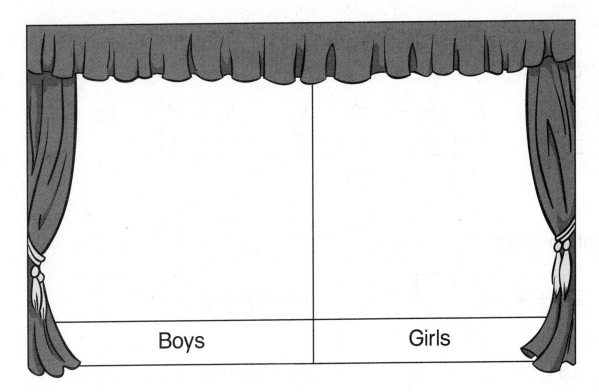

| Boys | Girls |

Write the number.

2. How many boys?

3. How many girls?

Compare the numbers in two ways.

4. [ ] > [ ]   [ ] < [ ]

Remembering

Add.

1. 4 +3	**2.** 6 +2	**3.** 8 +1	**4.** 5 +5	**5.** 2 +4

Subtract.

6. 10 − 4	**7.** 8 −5	**8.** 9 −8	**9.** 7 −1	**10.** 10 − 3

Count on to add.

11. $20 + 9 =$ ☐

12. $87 + 3 =$ ☐

13. $68 + 6 =$ ☐

14. $25 + 8 =$ ☐

15. ☐ $= 79 + 6$

16. ☐ $= 56 + 5$

17. Stretch Your Thinking Write a number
greater than 19 in Box A. Write a
number less than 99 in Box B.
Compare your numbers.

Box A   Box B